NATIONAL GEOGRAPHIC

Hurricanes

EXTREME WEATHER

Josie Green

PICTURE CREDITS
Cover: © Annie Griffiths Belt/Corbis

page 4 (bottom left) © Despotovic Dusko/Corbis Sygma; page 5 (top) © Getty Images; page 8 (left) © Tony Arruza/Corbis; page 9 (top) © AFP/Corbis; page 11 © Stocktrek/Corbis; page 13 (top) © Stock Image Group/SPL; page 13 (bottom) © Hubert Stadler/Corbis; page 16 © George Hall/Corbis; page 21 © Najlah Feanny/Corbis Saba; page 24 © Corbis Sygma; page 26 © Roger Ball/Corbis.

Produced through the worldwide resources of the National Geographic Society, John M. Fahey, Jr., President and Chief Executive Officer; Gilbert M. Grosvenor, Chairman of the Board.

PREPARED BY NATIONAL GEOGRAPHIC SCHOOL PUBLISHING
Sheron Long, Chief Executive Officer; Samuel Gesumaria, President; Steve Mico, Executive Vice President and Publisher; Francis Downey, Editor in Chief; Richard Easby, Editorial Manager; Margaret Sidlosky, Director of Design and Illustrations; Jim Hiscott, Design Manager; Cynthia Olson and Ruth Ann Thompson, Art Directors; Matt Wascavage, Director of Publishing Services; Lisa Pergolizzi, Production Manager.

MANUFACTURING AND QUALITY CONTROL
Christopher A. Liedel, Chief Financial Officer; Phillip L. Schlosser, Vice President; Clifton M. Brown III, Director.

EDITOR
Mary Anne Wengel

PROGRAMME CONSULTANTS
Dr. Shirley V. Dickson, National Literacy Consultant; James A. Shymansky, E. Desmond Lee Professor of Science Education, University of Missouri-St Louis.

McGraw-Hill International (UK) Limited
McGraw-Hill House
Shoppenhangers Road, Maidenhead
Berkshire, SL6 2QL

www.kingscourt.co.uk

ISBN–13: 978-1-4202-1714-8

Printed in Hong Kong.

2011 2010 2009 2008 2007
1 2 3 4 5 6 7 8 9 10 11 12 13 14 15

Contents

Extreme Weather

The weather affects people's lives in many different ways. Weather helps people decide what clothes to wear, or what to do in their spare time. However, the weather can also be a matter of life and death. Extreme weather can be very severe. Droughts, floods, tornadoes, and hurricanes are all examples of extreme weather.

 ## Key Concepts ....

1. Conditions in the atmosphere, such as air pressure, create weather.
2. Clouds give meteorologists clues about what is happening in the atmosphere.
3. Tools and technology help meteorologists gather data about weather.

Four Kinds of Extreme Weather

Droughts

Droughts happen when there is a lack of rain.

Floods

Floods happen when too much water flows over the land.

In this book you will learn about the causes and effects of hurricanes like this one.

Tornadoes

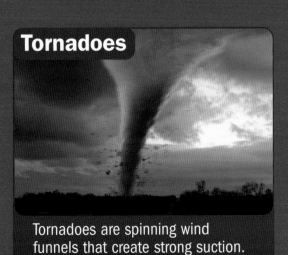

Tornadoes are spinning wind funnels that create strong suction.

Hurricanes

Hurricanes are powerful storms with strong winds and heavy rains.

Weather and Hurricanes

Imagine that you live near the ocean. You hear on the television news that a **hurricane** is on its way. First, the wind picks up and fast-moving clouds fill the sky. Next, giant waves batter the coast and some sweep inland. Then the storm itself reaches land. Raging winds rip roofs from houses and flatten buildings. Cars are overturned and telegraph poles are snapped in two. Heavy rains bring widespread flooding. By the time the storm has passed overhead and moved on, it has caused great destruction.

A Powerful Storm

A hurricane is a powerful storm that, from above, looks like a giant spinning wheel. It is made of swirling clouds and high winds. Hurricanes form over warm tropical waters and grow as warm moist air rises from the ocean to feed the storm.

The winds of a hurricane are very fast. They can reach speeds of 300 kilometers (185 miles) per hour. Hurricanes can also be very wide. They can measure up to 2,000 kilometers (1,243 miles) across.

Although hurricanes form over oceans, they often strike land. When they do, they can cause devastation. Their strong winds rip through towns and villages, wiping out buildings. Hurricanes can cause huge ocean waves to crash onto land, causing severe flooding. Every year, hurricanes destroy more property and kill more people than any other kind of extreme weather.

"Hurricane" is just one of the names given to these rotating tropical storms. Such storms are called hurricanes when they develop over the Atlantic Ocean and eastern Pacific Ocean. They are called typhoons in the northwest Pacific Ocean. Near Australia and in the Indian Ocean they are called tropical cyclones. No matter what they are called, all hurricane-type storms affect places mostly in the **tropics**. This is the area between the Tropic of Cancer and the Tropic of Capricorn.

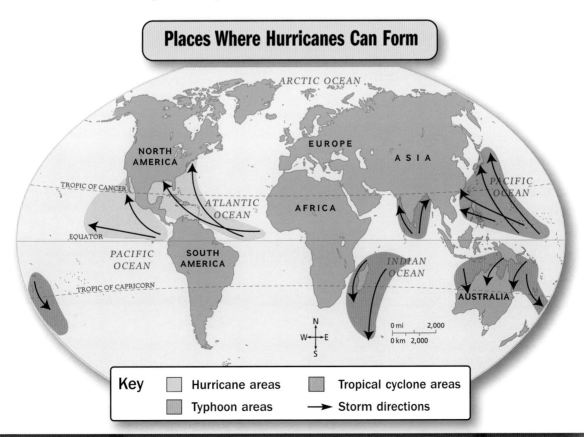

Places Where Hurricanes Can Form

| Key | ☐ Hurricane areas | ☐ Tropical cyclone areas |
| | ☐ Typhoon areas | → Storm directions |

Key Concept 1 Conditions in the atmosphere, such as air pressure, create weather.

Where Wind Comes From

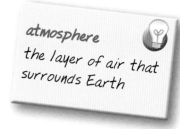

atmosphere
the layer of air that surrounds Earth

To understand what causes a hurricane, you first have to understand where wind comes from. Wind is created by changes in air pressure and temperature. Earth is surrounded by a layer of air called the **atmosphere**. This layer of air presses down on Earth's surface. This is called **air pressure**.

air pressure
the effect of air pressing down on Earth's surface

Air pressure is affected by temperature. When the sun heats the Earth, the air above the Earth is warmed. When a mass of air is warmed, it expands—its **particles** move apart. The expanding air becomes lighter, or less **dense**, and this lighter air rises. Because the warm air is rising away from the Earth, the air pressure on that area of the Earth is reduced. This creates an area of **low air pressure**.

When air is cooled, its particles move closer together. The air becomes heavier, or denser, so it sinks. The sinking, heavier air increases the air pressure on the Earth in that area. This creates an area of **high air pressure**.

Stormy weather is associated with low air pressure.

Clear weather is associated with high air pressure.

When sunlight strikes Earth's surface, it heats some areas of Earth more than other areas. This means that the air pressure is different in different areas of Earth. Because cool air is heavier than warm air, cool air from high-air-pressure areas always moves to replace rising warm air in low-air-pressure areas. This movement of air is what we call wind. The greater the difference in air pressure between two areas, the stronger the wind will blow.

Wind is the movement of air, caused by air pressure.

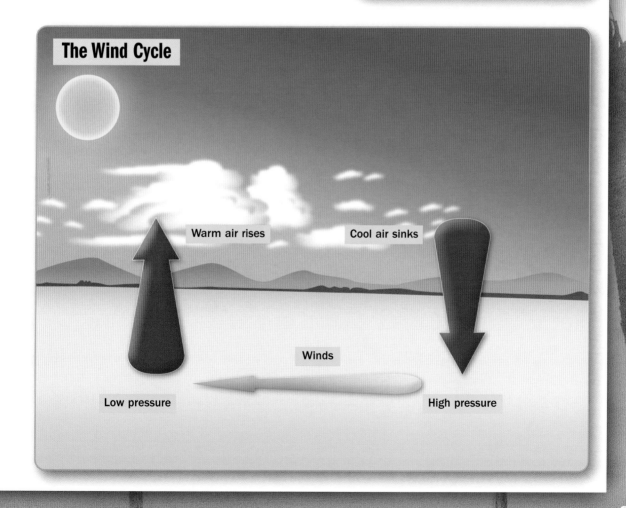

The Wind Cycle

Warm air rises

Cool air sinks

Winds

Low pressure

High pressure

Why Hurricanes Occur

There are two main weather conditions needed for a hurricane to form. One is a cold front. The other is high humidity.

Cold Front The first weather condition needed for a hurricane to form is a **front**. When a mass of warm moist air meets a mass of cold dry air a boundary called a front is formed. A cold front occurs when a mass of cold air is pushed under a warm air mass. This forces the warm air to rise. As the warm air rises it becomes cooler and condenses, forming clouds.

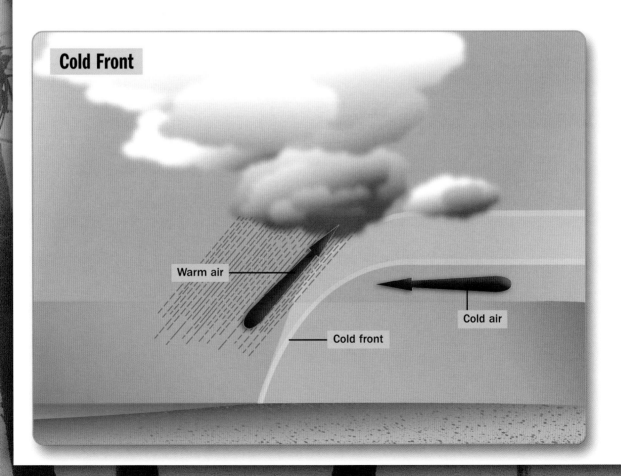

Cold Front

Warm air

Cold air

Cold front

High Humidity **Humidity** refers to the amount of water vapor in the air. High humidity means that the air contains a lot of water vapor. High humidity happens over the ocean when the sun heats the water, causing a large amount of water vapor to rise from the ocean, like steam from a tea kettle. This process is called **evaporation**. The temperature of the ocean's water must be over 26.5° Celsius (80° Fahrenheit) for the humidity to be high enough for a hurricane to form.

When a cold front creates low air pressure near the ocean surface, it begins to draw in humid air rising from the warm ocean water. Winds start to swirl around the low-air-pressure area. As the air pressure lowers further, more warm humid air is drawn in. The winds swirl faster. The rotation of Earth makes the warm winds travel in a spiral pattern around the low-air-pressure center. The winds spiral counterclockwise in the northern hemisphere and clockwise in the southern hemisphere.

As the storm travels across the ocean, it draws more and more energy and water from the warm, humid air. Eventually, the storm can grow into a huge swirling mass of cloud. When the wind speed reaches 119 kilometers (74 miles) per hour the storm is classed as a hurricane. The low-air-pressure center of this spiral is the eye of the hurricane. It stays calm.

The clouds of a hurricane form a swirling pattern.

Key Concept 2 Clouds give meteorologists clues about what is happening in the atmosphere.

Studying the Weather

Meteorologists are people who study weather. One way meteorologists can **forecast**, or predict, the weather is by looking at clouds. Clouds give important clues about what is happening in the atmosphere. Cumulus, cumulonimbus, and cirrus clouds may give meteorologists clues that a hurricane is developing.

Cumulus Clouds Cumulus clouds are puffy clouds that usually appear in clear weather. They look as soft as cotton balls, but they can grow and transform into violent storm clouds. Cumulus clouds form from rising columns of warm humid air. These clouds grow upward rather than across, so even though their bases are near the ground, they can grow to great heights.

Puffy cumulus clouds on a clear day

A towering cumulus cloud that looks like a cauliflower over the ocean is a clue that hurricane-producing storm clouds may form. This type of cumulus cloud can grow into a giant cumulonimbus storm cloud.

Cumulonimbus Clouds Cumulonimbus clouds are the tallest of all clouds. They can reach heights of 18,300 meters (60,000 feet). Because these clouds grow so tall, their tops form high up, where it is very cold. As a result, their tops are made up of ice crystals. The icy top of a cumulonimbus cloud spreads out into the shape of an anvil.

Rain falls from a cumulonimbus.

Anvil

If the conditions are right, thunderstorms that come from cumulonimbus clouds over the ocean can develop into hurricanes. During a hurricane, a cumulonimbus cloud can be enormous. It forms a distinct swirling shape as it is blown by the winds of the hurricane.

Cirrus Clouds Cirrus clouds form high up, where it is very cold, so they are made up of ice crystals. Cirrus clouds appear thin and wispy. They usually form during clear weather, but they can be a sign that bad weather is coming. The presence of long cirrus clouds may be the first sign of a developing hurricane.

Cirrus clouds are often present during a hurricane, too. As warm air escapes from the eye of the hurricane, it freezes and forms cirrus clouds above the hurricane.

Key Concept 3 Tools and technology help meteorologists gather data about weather.

Predicting Hurricanes

Meteorologists can predict hurricanes by studying weather conditions. They use special tools and instruments to collect weather **data**, or information. Computers at weather offices analyze the data and turn it into weather maps, which can be used to forecast a hurricane. Nothing can be done to stop a hurricane, but meteorologists can track the storm and predict where it will go next. This way, they can warn people before a hurricane strikes.

Meteorologists use many tools to collect weather data. These include weather satellites, radar, and weather planes.

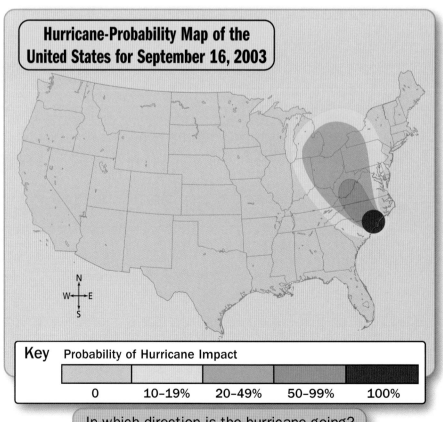

Hurricane-Probability Map of the United States for September 16, 2003

Key Probability of Hurricane Impact

| 0 | 10–19% | 20–49% | 50–99% | 100% |

In which direction is the hurricane going?

Weather Satellites   Weather satellites orbit Earth in space. Some of these satellites orbit 35,400 kilometers (22,000 miles) above the Equator. They take photographs of Earth's weather, including storms. The photographs are beamed back to Earth. Meteorologists study cloud development and movement by comparing a series of photographs to work out the speed and direction of hurricanes. Satellites can also keep track of low-pressure areas that might lead to a hurricane developing.

This satellite photograph shows swirling hurricane clouds.

Radar   Radar is also used to track a hurricane. Most radar has a limited range and is most useful for watching hurricanes within 240 kilometers (150 miles) of land. Some radar stations are mounted on buildings and some are mounted on trucks.

An antenna connected to a dish sends out radio waves. These waves reflect off water in clouds and travel back to the antenna. Pictures of the clouds are created from the waves. These pictures can tell experts about the strength of the storm. They can also show in which direction the hurricane is moving.

Weather Planes Special weather planes travel through storm clouds to collect data. They carry tools under their wings or on their noses. These tools measure temperature, air pressure, and wind speed.

In the United States, planes called "hurricane hunters" fly over and around hurricanes to observe their progress. Some of these planes fly right into the eye of the storm. Meteorologists learn about the nature of hurricanes from the data gathered by these planes.

A "hurricane hunter" weather plane, used to collect data on hurricanes

During the Hurricane During the hurricane, meteorologists rate the strength of the storm. To do this, they use the **Saffir-Simpson scale**. The rating is worked out on wind speeds and by how much the sea level rises. The highest rating on the Saffir-Simpson scale is category 5. Hurricanes of this scale reach wind speeds of 251 kilometers (156 miles) per hour or more. They raise the sea level over 5.8 meters (19 feet).

Think About the Key Concepts

Think about what you read. Think about the pictures and diagrams. Use these to answer the questions. Share what you think with others.

1. Name one kind of extreme weather. What conditions lead to this weather?

2. What can meteorologists learn about the weather from studying clouds?

3. What tools do meteorologists use to forecast the weather?

4. How does extreme weather affect people and the land?

Weather Maps

Weather maps contain information that helps you understand the weather.

Look back at the weather map on page 14. It is a weather map of the United States that shows the probability of a hurricane hitting a certain area.

The weather map on page 19 is a different kind of weather map. It shows the weather conditions surrounding a tropical cyclone approaching northeast Australia. To read a weather map, follow the steps below.

How to Read a Weather Map

1. **Read the title to learn what the map shows.**
   What is this weather map about?

2. **Read the key to learn what the symbols stand for.**
   What do the lines show? What do the letters L and H stand for?

3. **Study the information on the map.**
   Which towns do you think the tropical cyclone will affect? What facts helped you form your opinion?

4. **Think about what you have learned.**
   If clear weather was likely in a city, what would you expect to see on the map?

Tropical Cyclone Conditions in Australia

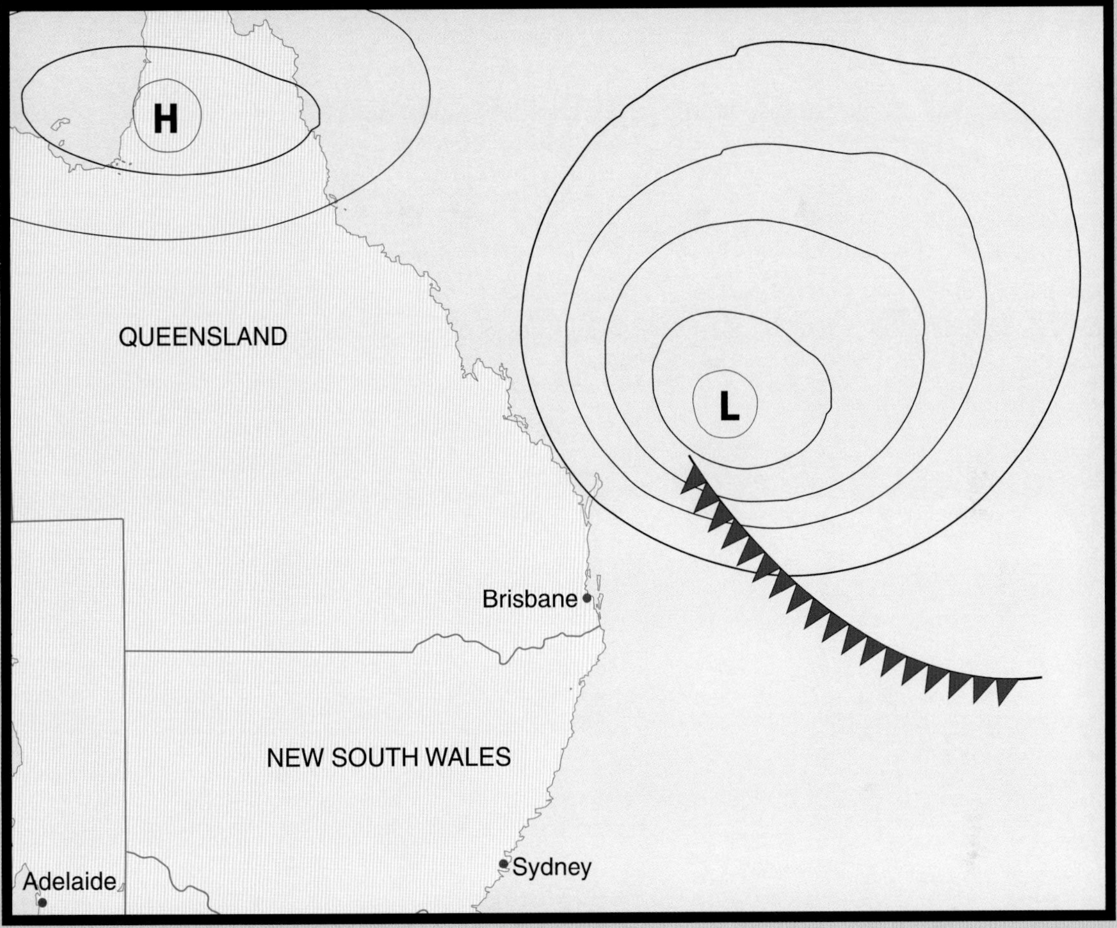

H

QUEENSLAND

L

Brisbane

NEW SOUTH WALES

Adelaide

Sydney

Key

L Area of low air pressure

H Area of high air pressure

▲▲ Cold front – cold air meets and is pushed under warm air

╱ Isobars – join areas that have the same air pressure

Explanations

An **explanation** can tell how and why something happened. The article starting on page 21 tells about one specific weather event. It explains what happened, why it happened, and what effects it had on the people and land.

An explanation includes the following:

The Introduction
The introduction gives the reader an overview, or the big picture of what the explanation is about.

Body Paragraphs
The body paragraphs make up most of the writing in the explanation. They provide the information and details that help to explain the event.

The Conclusion
The conclusion summarizes or ties together the information in the explanation.

Hurricane Andrew, August 1992

The **title** tells you the topic.

Hurricanes in the United States usually occur in the hurricane season, between June and October. The southeastern states of the United States are often at risk from hurricanes at this time. In August 1992, the states of Florida, Louisiana, and Mississippi were hit by a very destructive hurricane, Hurricane Andrew.

The **introduction** tells you what the explanation will be about.

Andrew caused a lot of damage. It ripped houses apart, flattened trees, and ruined crops. People had no power and no drinking water. Many people lost everything they owned, and some people lost their lives. It was the costliest natural disaster in American history.

Maps, diagrams, charts, and **photographs** help you picture what you are reading.

This house in Florida was destroyed by Hurricane Andrew.

Causes of Hurricanes in the United States

Body paragraphs give details.

The southeastern states of the United States are sometimes hit by hurricanes. Hurricanes are strong storms that begin over warm oceans. The surface of the water must be very warm for a hurricane to form, so hurricanes mostly form over tropical oceans.

Most of the hurricanes that affect the United States form in one of three places. These places are the Gulf of Mexico, the western Caribbean Sea, and near the Cape Verde Islands, off the east coast of Africa.

Many of the strongest hurricanes develop in the Cape Verde area. They develop from fronts caused by hot air blowing from the Sahara Desert. A front forms when hot air moves west and meets cooler air over the coast of Africa. The evaporation of the warm water in the Atlantic Ocean near the Cape Verde Islands provides the energy for the storms to develop. As these storms start to develop, strong winds move them west toward North and South America. Hurricane Andrew, which hit the southeastern United States in 1992, was one such hurricane.

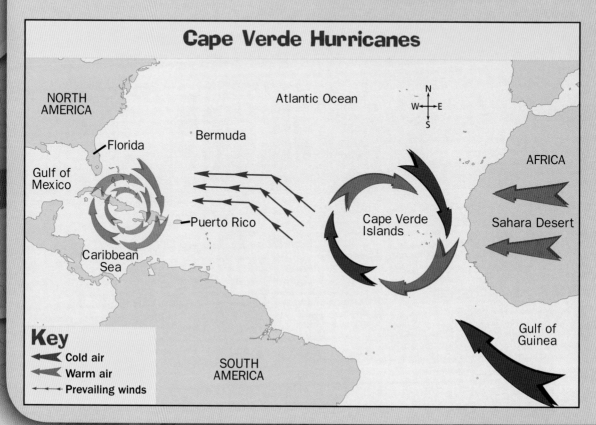

Cape Verde Hurricanes

NORTH AMERICA

Atlantic Ocean

N
W — E
S

Florida

Bermuda

Gulf of Mexico

AFRICA

Cape Verde Islands

Sahara Desert

Puerto Rico

Caribbean Sea

Gulf of Guinea

Key
- Cold air
- Warm air
- Prevailing winds

SOUTH AMERICA

How Hurricane Andrew Began

Hurricane Andrew began to form in the Cape Verde area on August 16, 1992. First, the lower warm air gathered together and rose. This caused cumulus clouds and winds to develop. A storm called a tropical depression developed. A tropical depression is a storm that has lighter winds than a hurricane.

On the next day, August 17, the tropical depression became Tropical Storm Andrew. This meant the storm had increased in strength, but its winds had not yet reached hurricane intensity. The storm was quickly moving northwest over the Atlantic.

By August 21, Andrew was midway between Bermuda and Puerto Rico and still increasing in strength. By this time, a high-pressure area had developed over the United States. Winds from the high-pressure area caused Andrew to turn westward towards Florida.

On August 22, Andrew's winds increased to hurricane strength. The United States Weather Office issued a hurricane warning for the Bahamas and a hurricane watch for eastern Florida.

This time lapse satellite photograph shows three stages of Hurricane Andrew as it approached the United States.

Andrew Heads for the United States

On August 23 and 24, Andrew passed over the Bahamas, killing three people and causing 250 million dollars worth of damages. The weather office changed the hurricane watch for eastern Florida to a hurricane warning.

After sweeping over the Bahamas, Andrew strengthened again as it crossed the Straits of Florida. When Andrew hit Homestead, Florida, it was a category 4 hurricane on the Saffir-Simpson scale. The winds were blowing up to 229 kilometers per hour (142 miles per hour).

Andrew took about four hours to pass over southern Florida. It weakened slightly over the land, but strengthened again over the warm waters of the Gulf of Mexico. Then, air currents steered Andrew northwest towards Louisiana.

The Saffir-Simpson Scale

Category	Wind Speed	
	kilometers per hour	miles per hour
1	119–153	74–95
2	154–177	96–110
3	178–209	111–130
4	210–250	131–155
5	251+	156+

On August 26, Andrew hit the coast of Louisiana. By now it was weakening and was only a category 3 hurricane. Even so, it brought nearly 30 centimeters (12 inches) of rain to Hammond, Louisiana. It also caused the high tide to be 2.5 meters (8 feet) higher than usual. In southeastern Louisiana the hurricane produced a tornado that left a path of damage 14.5 kilometers (9 miles) long.

The effects of Hurricane Andrew on Louisiana

Hurricane Andrew Dies Out

Hurricanes need a large amount of warm, moist air to fuel them. Once a hurricane reaches land it is cut off from this fuel supply and begins to weaken. Hurricane Andrew soon weakened to tropical storm status once it reached land in Louisiana. After another 12 hours, Andrew was only a tropical depression again. However, the storm still caused heavy rainfall for the areas beneath it.

By midday on August 28, Andrew had virtually disappeared. But the storm left devastation behind.

Hurricane Andrew above Louisiana

The Path of Hurricane Andrew

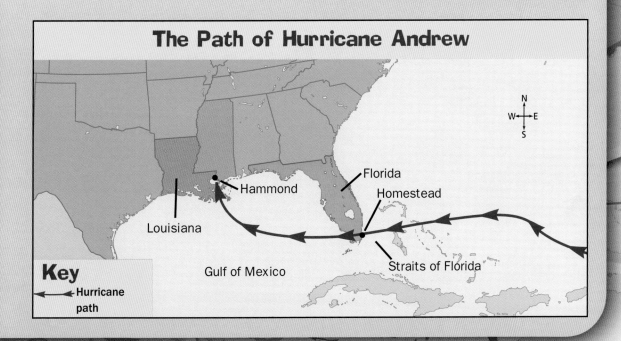

N
W—E
S

Florida

Homestead

Hammond

Louisiana

Straits of Florida

Gulf of Mexico

Key

←—← Hurricane path

The Effects of Hurricane Andrew

The **conclusion** summarizes the text.

In its few days of life, Hurricane Andrew caused devastation to the Bahamas, Florida, Louisiana, and Mississippi. The hurricane caused over 25 billion dollars worth of damages, and killed 26 people.

About 600,000 homes and businesses were destroyed or badly damaged by Andrew's winds, rain, and waves. Hundreds of thousands of people were left without homes or power for up to six months.

Hurricane Andrew was the most expensive natural disaster to ever hit the United States. It took months to repair the damage. The disaster was a terrible reminder of how little power people have in the face of extreme weather.

The aftermath of Hurricane Andrew in Florida

Apply the Key Concepts

Key Concept 1 Conditions in the atmosphere, such as air pressure, create weather.

Activity Research more information about the weather conditions that produce hurricanes. A good place to start is to find out where most Atlantic hurricanes start. Look on the Internet or in books in the library. Make a list of the weather conditions in areas where hurricanes are born.

Weather Conditions
1. high humidity
2.
3.

Key Concept 2 Clouds give meteorologists clues about what is happening in the atmosphere.

Activity Draw a chart with three columns. In the first column, draw pictures of the different kinds of clouds related to hurricanes. In the second, name each kind of cloud and describe what it looks like. In the third, explain what each cloud tells about the weather. Label your chart with a title that summarizes its contents.

My Title

Key Concept 3 Tools and technology help meteorologists gather data about weather.

Activity Use the Internet or the library to find out more about the instruments that meteorologists use to track hurricanes. How does radar help meteorologists predict the path of a hurricane? How do meteorologists know when to issue a hurricane watch or a hurricane warning? Write a short account of your findings.

Hurricane Tracking
_____
_____
_____

Create
Your Own
Explanation

There are lots of examples of extreme weather around the world. Some extreme weather may even happen close to where you live. Can you remember a flood or a drought? Can you remember a big storm that turned into a hurricane or caused a tornado?

1. Study the Model

Look back at the description of explanations on page 20. Then, read the article on pages 21–26 again. Look for the examples in the text that tell you this is an explanation. Can you find the opening statement? Can you find the concluding statement? Which paragraphs explain the causes of the weather disaster? Which paragraphs explain the effects of the weather disaster? Look at the diagrams or maps again. Think about how they helped you understand the topic.

2. Choose Your Topic

Now choose one example of an extreme weather event that you would like to find out more about. You may have to start by looking at books on extreme weather, reading newspaper accounts, or using the Internet. Once you've chosen your topic, you're ready to start.

3. Research Your Topic

Ask yourself what you already know about this topic. Do you know enough to write an explanation of how or why it occurred? Probably not. So, you need to make a list of questions that you will answer. Remember that you are going to write an explanation, so many of your questions may start with "how" or "why." Now go to the library or to the Internet to get your facts.

Monsoon

1. What caused the monsoon?

2. How did the monsoon affect people?

4. Take Notes

Take notes of what you find out. As you find out a new fact, you may find that it leads to another question. Write the new questions down so that you don't forget them. As you write your notes, make a note of the things that you can explain using a diagram or map.

5. Write a Draft

Look back at the facts you found. Do they explain how or why your event occurred? If they do, start writing your draft. You may need to check back with page 20 to remind yourself of the features of an explanation.

6. Revise and Edit

Reread your draft. Does it explain your extreme weather event? Does it have all the features of an explanation? Have you spelled special weather words correctly? Have you drawn charts and maps to help with the explanation?

Present Your Explanation

Now you can share your work. With a group of students, present your explanations as part of a television special report on extreme weather. The program will be called *Explaining Extreme Weather*.

How to Present Your Work

1. **Choose a person in your group to be the anchorperson.**
   That person will introduce each member of the group. The anchorperson will also read the opening statement from each explanation.

2. **Collect the equipment you will need.**
   Before you make your presentation, you will need to transfer your charts and maps to overhead transparencies or to a piece of poster board.

3. **Rehearse your reading.**
   Before you read your explanation you will need to rehearse reading it aloud. Read it aloud several times. Practice looking up at your audience while you are speaking.

4. **When you have finished, be prepared to answer questions.**
   Your audience may ask you to explain something in more detail or review some of the facts.

5. **When you have all made your oral presentations, bind the explanations together and make them into a book.**
   As a group, make a cover for the book. Then, bind all the pages together with staples or yarn.

Hailstorms

Hailstorms can cause damage all over the world.

2

Worst Hailstorms

Some of the worst hailstorms have occurred at these places.

3

Glossary

air pressure – the effect of air pressing down on Earth's surface

atmosphere – the layer of air that surrounds Earth

data – information that is collected

dense – the result of particles being very close together, making a substance thick or heavy

evaporation – the process where water warms up and turns into vapor

forecast – to predict what the weather will be like

front – a weather condition that occurs when areas of air with different temperatures meet

high air pressure – a weather condition that occurs when there is a lot of air pressing down on Earth

humidity – the amount of moisture in the air

hurricane – a severe storm that starts over warm seawater and brings strong winds, heavy rain, and huge waves

low air pressure – a weather condition that occurs when there is not much air pressing down on Earth

meteorologists – scientists who study the weather

particles – very small parts of a substance that cannot be seen with the eye alone

Saffir-Simpson scale – a scale that rates hurricanes depending on their wind speed and how much the sea level rises

tropics – the area between the Tropic of Cancer and the Tropic of Capricorn, where the oceans are warm

Index